**DATE DUE**

| | | | |
|---|---|---|---|
| OCT 2 1 1997 | | | |
| | | | |
| | | | |
| | | | |
| | | | |
| | | | |
| | | | |
| | | | |
| | | | |
| | | | |
| | | | |

# AIDS

Look for these and other books in the Lucent Overview series:

# AIDS

by Jonnie Wilson

LUCENT
B·O·O·K·S

LUCENT Overview Series

# LUCENT Overview Series

**Library of Congress Cataloging-in-Publication Data**

Wilson, Jonnie, 1938-
     AIDS / by Jonnie Wilson.
        p.    cm. — (Lucent overview series)
     Bibliography: p.
     Includes index.
     Summary: Examines the current and future outlook on AIDS,
how it can be prevented, how it affects the body, and what is being
done regarding patients with the disease.
     ISBN 1-56006-105-7
     1. AIDS (Disease)—Juvenile literature.   [1. AIDS (Disease)]
I. Title.  II. Series.
RC607.A26W55   1989
616.97'92—dc20

89-12619
CIP
AC

© Copyright 1989 by Lucent Books, Inc.
P.O. Box 289011, San Diego, CA 92128-9011

# Contents

CHAPTER ONE

# AIDS: The Deadly Disease

In 1981, several hundred people in the United States came down with a strange disease that was so new it didn't even have a name. Doctors didn't know then where it came from, what was causing it, or how to treat it. What they did know was that it was killing people. Many more became sick. By April 1989, the deadly disease had been responsible for the deaths of over fifty-four thousand people. By this time, it had a name, a name familiar to almost everyone in the country—AIDS.

## What is AIDS?

AIDS, or Acquired Immune Deficiency Syndrome, is a fatal disease that is caused by a virus. Because AIDS is a new disease, many people are confused about what it is and how it is caused. Some are overly concerned for their safety. Others don't think AIDS affects them at all. Perhaps some have heard that only homosexual men (gays) get the disease. Statistics show, however, that anyone can become infected with the AIDS virus *under the right circumstances*. People with AIDS are male or female, rich or poor. They are married or single, young or old, and represent all races. Researchers think that by the end of 1992, more than 260,000 people in the United States will have died from complications of this tragic illness.

As of now, there is no cure for AIDS, nor is there a vaccine to prevent healthy people from becoming infected with the AIDS virus. Since 1981, billions of dollars have been spent on research to find ways to eliminate this health threat. Despite these efforts, it is unlikely that any major medical breakthroughs will occur within the next ten years. At present, treatment for AIDS patients focuses on providing drugs that slow down the progress of the disease. Drugs are also used to treat or prevent other infections. Such treatments can prolong a patient's life, but are unable to rid the body of the virus.

The most important thing to know about AIDS is that it can be prevented. One's best protection is learning what is now known about how the virus is transmitted and keeping informed as new findings are revealed. Education is society's only "vaccine" against this devastating disease.

## Where did AIDS come from?

No one is absolutely sure how or where AIDS began. Because AIDS has been a serious health problem in Africa for a long time, some researchers think the disease started there. It may have been introduced to humans by the green monkey of central Africa. Scientists have found that almost half of these monkeys carry a virus similar to the one that causes AIDS. Although this virus is harmless to the monkeys, it may have changed into a deadly form once it entered the human population. According to this theory, Africans may have become infected through monkey bites or through the eating of monkey meat. Then the virus could have spread as Africans traveled about and visitors to Africa returned to their own countries.

Although the first AIDS cases were diagnosed in 1981, scientists believe the disease may have existed as early as 1959. They think this because a stored sample of blood taken from an African in 1959 was tested in the 1980s and found to be infected with the AIDS virus. As of 1989, AIDS has been diagnosed in 149 countries in the world. It is present in every state of the United States. However, about half of the AIDS patients in this country live in California and New York. All cases of AIDS in the United States are reported to the Centers for Disease Control (CDC) in Atlanta, Georgia. The CDC, an agency of the United States government, gathers information on outbreaks of unusual and contagious diseases. The agency also plans programs of prevention and control.

## AIDS and HIV infection

AIDS is caused by the human immunodeficiency virus (HIV). Unlike such diseases as the blood disorder hemophilia, it cannot be inherited. Nor can AIDS result from a malfunction of the body as happens in diabetes. Rather, AIDS is an *acquired* disease. To get AIDS, a person must have intimate contact with a person who is already infected with HIV.

*A blood bank technician places units of donated blood in a refrigerated room. Blood banks depend on the generosity of the public to keep the supply of blood sufficient to meet medical demands.*

Being infected with the AIDS virus is not the same thing as having AIDS. HIV may live in a person's body for many years without causing problems. Those people who are infected with HIV, but who do not have any AIDS-related symptoms, are called asymptomatic carriers. Symptoms or not, anyone who is infected with HIV is able to spread the virus to another person under the right circumstances. Carriers often look and feel healthy. As a result, they may be quite unaware they carry the virus. This is one of the main reasons HIV has been able to spread so quickly in many areas.

As of mid-1989, about 100,000 people had been diagnosed with AIDS in the United States. Researchers believe, however, that the total number of people *infected with HIV* may be as high as 1.5

million. These people will remain infected for the rest of their lives because once HIV enters the body, it does not leave. In the absence of a cure, research shows that most people who are now infected with HIV will go on to develop AIDS.

## Transmission of the AIDS virus HIV

HIV is transmitted through intimate contact with infected body fluids. Primarily these fluids are blood, semen, and vaginal secretions. The virus is most often spread through sexual intercourse or through the sharing of intravenous (IV) drug equipment.

## Sexual contact

Normally the skin provides an effective barrier against disease-carrying microorganisms such as HIV. (Microorganisms are tiny living creatures, such as bacteria and viruses, that affect the body.) However, HIV can easily enter the body if infected fluids come in contact with breaks or tears in the skin. For instance, a woman could become infected through sexual intercourse if she has any sores or tears in the skin inside her vagina. If her sexual partner is infected, the virus in his semen could enter her body through these tiny openings. Women are often unaware of such tears and sores. Generally they are hidden from view and may not be painful. There is also some evidence that mucous membrane, the type of tissue that lines the vagina, may not provide as much protection as external skin. HIV may be able to pass through this tissue even if there are no tears or sores.

It is also possible for a man to acquire HIV through sexual intercourse with an infected woman. The virus could get into the man's body through a break in the skin or a sore on his penis if he is exposed to infected vaginal secretions. It may even be possible for HIV to gain entrance through the mucous membrane tissue that lines the inside of the penis.

The most risky type of sexual contact is anal intercourse. This type of intercourse involves a man inserting his penis into his partner's anus. Such sexual contact is very risky because the mucous membrane tissue inside the anus is delicate and tears easily. The virus in infected semen can gain entrance to the body in the same ways as in vaginal intercourse. Anal intercourse can occur between a man and a woman or between a man and another man. During the early 1980s, many homosexual and bisexual men became infected this way. About two-thirds of all people who have contracted AIDS in the United States have been homosexual or bisexual men.

Prostitutes, particularly those in large cities, are at high risk for becoming infected with the AIDS virus. Most prostitutes are women. But some young men—particularly homeless runaways—take part in prostitution, too. Runaway teenage boys often resort to prostitution with men to make money to survive on the streets. Whether male

*A prostitute is arrested by plainclothes policemen in Times Square in New York City. Prostitutes are a high-risk group for contracting and spreading AIDS because of their high number of sexual partners.*

or female, prostitutes are at high risk of becoming infected with HIV because they generally have many sexual partners. The more sexual partners a person has, the more likely he or she will come into contact with someone who is infected.

In most of the AIDS cases, sexual intercourse (vaginal and anal) has been responsible for transmission of the virus. Some researchers, however, think there is also a possibility that HIV can be transmitted through oral sex. Oral sex involves mouth and tongue contact with a partner's genitals. During oral sex, HIV from infected semen and vaginal secretions could enter a person's bloodstream through tears or sores on the inside of the mouth. Also, this tissue is mucous membrane. The AIDS virus may be able to pass through it.

Very small amounts of HIV have also been found in the saliva of some infected people. So far, however, it has not been proven that any cases of HIV infection have been transmitted by this body fluid.

One thing that is known for certain is that once a person becomes infected with HIV, he or she is infected for life. This means the person will be able to spread the disease to any and all future sexual partners.

## Intravenous (IV) drugs

Using intravenous drugs (shooting up) is the second most common way of becoming infected with HIV. Intravenous drug users use needles to inject drugs such as cocaine and heroin into their veins. They risk infection if they share needles with others because many drug users do not disinfect their needles between uses. Sometimes a small amount of a person's blood remains in or on the needle after shooting up. If that person is infected, HIV could be passed directly into the bloodstream of the next person who uses the needle. HIV infection through IV drug use has increased greatly since 1986. In 1988, IV drug use was linked to almost one-third of all AIDS cases.

IV drug users are particularly vulnerable to AIDS because the drugs they inject weaken the immune system. This makes it easier for in-

*Young addicts shoot up drugs in the doorway of an abandoned building. Intravenous-drug users often share needles with other users. If one user is infected with the AIDS virus, he or she can infect everyone else who uses the same needle.*

fection to take place. IV drug users face many other health risks, too. Hepatitis B (a disease of the liver) and malaria are two other diseases that can be transmitted intravenously. And because many prostitutes are also IV drug users, people in this group may be exposed daily to the two main sources of infection: sex and IV needles.

## Other methods of transmission

Sexual contact and IV drug use account for most cases of HIV infection. However, some people became infected through blood transfusions they received before March 1985. Each year, more than fourteen million pints of blood are collected at blood banks in the United States. Most people who receive this blood are accident victims or surgery patients. Donated blood has aided in the recovery of many patients and has saved a great number of lives. In the early years of the AIDS epidemic, however, a small number of people received blood that could actually cause them harm. The donated blood was infected with HIV. Tragically, long after they had recovered from their surgery or accident, some of these people became ill with AIDS.

People with hemophilia were especially affected in the early 1980s. Hemophilia is an inherited condition in which a person's blood does not clot properly. Because even small cuts can cause life-threatening bleeding in hemophiliacs, the condition is sometimes called "bleeder's disease." To live a normal life, a hemophiliac frequently needs transfusions of Factor VIII. This is a blood product that has certain proteins the hemophiliac lacks.

Factor VIII is a concentrated product made from plasma, the liquid portion of blood. A single pint of Factor VIII may have plasma from as many as 2,500-10,000 donors. This means that hemophiliacs are exposed to the blood of thousands of donors each year. Before March

*Donors give blood in an Atlanta, Georgia, plasma center. Fear of contracting AIDS has prevented many donors from giving blood and many recipients from accepting donated blood. But the AIDS virus can now be detected in donated blood.*

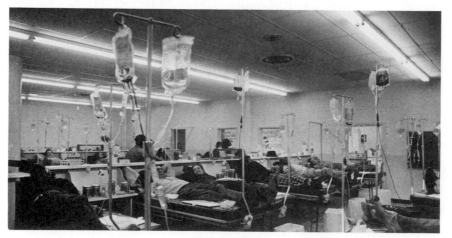

1985, this exposure often had tragic results. As many as 80 percent of hemophiliacs in some areas may now be infected with HIV as a result of infected Factor VIII received years ago. Factor VIII presently undergoes a heat treatment process that destroys the HIV virus.

Since March 1985, all blood donations have been tested for the presence of HIV. Any blood found to be infected is destroyed. To make sure that most blood is safe when collected, donors are asked questions about their health and behaviors. Only healthy people who say they have not participated in high-risk activities, such as sharing IV needles, are allowed to give blood.

## Little risk from donations

Most experts agree that today there is very little risk involved in receiving donated blood. The chance of becoming infected with HIV through a blood transfusion is estimated to be about one in 100,000. People who are concerned about the safety of the blood supply and who are scheduled to have surgery can donate their own blood for later use. This is called autologous (related to self) transfusion.

The last proven way HIV is spread involves the tiniest of AIDS victims: babies. An infected pregnant woman can pass the virus to her child before or during birth. She can also possibly pass the virus to her baby through infected breast milk. About half of the babies born to infected mothers carry the virus. Since the mother may not look or feel sick when she gets pregnant, she may not know she is endangering the life of her unborn child. Babies are particularly susceptible to the effects of the virus. This is probably because babies' immune systems are not fully developed. Infected babies weaken quickly and rarely live beyond two years. In a recent study, it was found that one out of every sixty-one babies born in New York City hospitals was infected. Most of these babies were born to mothers who were either IV drug users or the sexual partners of IV drug users.

The pregnancy may also be risky for the mother. Having a baby can weaken an infected woman and make her more likely to develop

*A demonstrator at an AIDS rally in Washington, D.C., is arrested. The police officers making the arrest are wearing rubber gloves to protect themselves from possible contact with AIDS-infected body fluids.*

AIDS. For a woman who already has AIDS, another tragedy may follow: she may be too sick to care for her newborn child.

## Casual contact

The AIDS virus cannot make a person sick unless it can get into that person's bloodstream. Infection is known to occur through exposure to infected body fluids. According to researchers, however, there is no evidence that the virus can be transmitted through casual contact. That is, one cannot get AIDS from being in the same room with an infected person or by touching him or her. Nor can AIDS be acquired by handling objects that belong to an infected person.

Health professionals have good reason for believing this. There have been no known cases of family members getting the disease through being around a loved one with AIDS. (This does not apply, of course, to a person who is sexually intimate with the patient.) Nor have friends and co-workers who have regular contact with an AIDS patient become infected.

## Other concerns

Some persons are afraid they may become infected if they donate blood. This is a needless worry. Blood banks always use new needles when they collect blood. Also, all medical supplies are delivered in sealed, sterile containers. Needles are used once and then thrown away to prevent others from coming in contact with the donor's blood.

Another needless fear is that of catching AIDS from an insect bite. It is true that some diseases, such as malaria, are spread in this way. The latest research, however, shows that HIV is not transmitted by mosquitos, fleas, or other insects. Nor is it spread through food, water, or air. This means people needn't stay away from restaurants, public gatherings, or even community swimming pools for fear of catching AIDS. It also means they won't become infected if someone sneezes on them.

A few people in the medical community are not satisfied with current research. They feel there is still too much to be learned about AIDS to say it can't be spread in this way or that. Yet all major health organizations, including the U.S. Public Health Service, agree that infection does not take place through casual contact. If the disease were easily transmitted, researchers say, most people in the world would have it by now.

CHAPTER TWO

# The AIDS Virus and Its Effect on the Body

HIV, the virus that causes AIDS, wasn't discovered until 1983. Other viruses have been around for a very long time. They cause diseases such as polio, chicken pox, and the common cold. Some viruses even attack plants and animals. For example, a virus is responsible for a serious cat disease called feline leukemia.

Viruses are much smaller than other disease-causing organisms. They are so small they cannot be seen under an ordinary microscope. In fact, it was not until the electron microscope was invented in 1931 that viruses were observed for the first time.

The fact that viruses are small gave doctors the first clue that a virus was causing AIDS in hemophiliacs. Because bacteria and other germs are much larger than viruses, they can be filtered out of Factor VIII, the blood product needed by hemophiliacs. But viruses are so small they pass through the filter. This is why doctors suspected a virus as the cause of AIDS when hemophiliacs first started coming down with the disease. They knew that only tiny viruses could have stayed in the Factor VIII after the filtering process.

Viruses are extremely hard to get rid of once they have entered the body. Antibiotics, drugs that can kill bacteria, have no effect on viruses. And medications that are strong enough to kill a virus are also strong enough to kill body cells that the virus has infected. Because of this, there is often no safe treatment for a viral disease.

Viruses are different from other germs in another important way. They cannot reproduce by themselves. To reproduce, a virus must first find a living cell, called a host cell, to get the materials the virus needs. In order to find a host cell, the virus must be able to get inside a living organism (human, animal, or plant).

Most viruses that cause human diseases are able to harm only one part of the body or one body system. For example, the polio virus is able to attack only cells of the central nervous system. Viruses that cause the common cold, on the other hand, can infect only the respiratory system (nose, throat, and lungs).

What makes a virus attack only one particular part of the body? The answer lies in the virus's outer shell of protein. This protein shell is shaped to fit exactly an outer part of the kind of cell it attacks. The parts must match perfectly, as in a jigsaw puzzle, or the virus will not be able to pass through the cell wall. This is why the polio virus cannot damage the cells in a person's stomach, liver, or kidneys. Since its shell matches only those of central nervous system cells, these are the only cells it can attack.

## The immune system

We live in a world of germs. They are in the air we breathe, the food we eat, and the water we drink. But most germs don't make us sick because of a special part of our body called the immune system. This system's job is to keep us healthy by fighting off germs that are able to invade our bodies.

The immune system is extremely complex. Much is still to be learned about its special cells and their many intricate connections. Some scientists think that the immune system is almost as complex as the human brain. Bone marrow, lymph nodes, lymph vessels, the spleen, the thymus gland, and white blood cells are all part of the immune system.

T-cells, special kinds of white blood cells, circulate in the bloodstream. They play a vital role in disease prevention. These cells

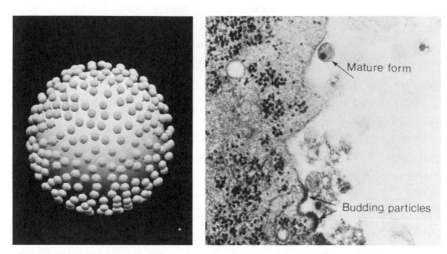

*Richard Feldmann of the National Institutes of Health used a computer to produce the model of the human immunovirus (HIV) shown at left. The photo on the right shows a human T-cell infected with HIV. The virus first produces "buds" on the T-cell, which then mature into fully developed immunoviruses.*

have the ability to distinguish between the body's own tissue (self) and foreign cells (nonself). When T-cells come in contact with germs in the bloodstream, they send messages to other white blood cells to join in the fight against these foreigners. Among those who hurry to the rescue are macrophages, whose job is to gobble up viruses and other germs. Other body defenders called natural killer cells help by releasing a poison that is able to kill invading germs.

Also called upon by the T-cells are B-lymphocyte cells. These cells produce special substances called antibodies, which help the white blood cells destroy the invading germ. After they have done their job, the antibodies stay in the bloodstream. There they are able to prevent future attacks by the same kind of germ. This is why once people have had a certain disease, such as measles or chicken pox, they will not get that disease again. Antibodies are able to give this protection.

As is true with other viruses, HIV can attack only certain body cells. But this virus is especially dangerous because it attacks the cells in the system designed to keep us well: the immune system. HIV is able to do this because its outer protein shell perfectly matches a protein molecule found on the outside of T-cells. This match makes it possible for the virus to enter these cells and use them to produce more viruses. Each infected host cell eventually makes thousands of new viruses. As the cell weakens and dies, the viruses are released into the bloodstream. There they seek out other T-cells to attack.

HIV is a dangerous invader for another reason: it can outsmart the antibodies the body produces to destroy it. With most illnesses,

*At left is an electron micrograph of normal human T-cells. T-cells are the watchdogs of the body's immune system. They can recognize the presence of invading viruses or germs in the bloodstream, and then call in killer cells to destroy the invaders. At right is a T-cell infected with HIV (white area).*

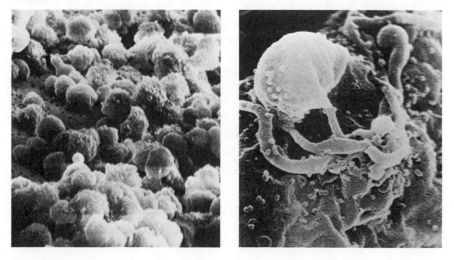

a weakened body returns to good health once the antibodies have defeated the invading germ. However, in the case of HIV, the immune system's antibodies are ineffective. For reasons not yet understood, they cannot stop the virus from spreading.

Researchers think one reason the antibodies can't stop the virus is they can't find it. It hides deep inside the host T-cells. Also, HIV has the ability to mutate, or change its shape. When mutation occurs, the antibodies can no longer recognize the new shape as the virus to attack.

## How the disease develops

It takes anywhere from several weeks to six months after exposure to HIV for a person's body to produce antibodies against this virus. (But even before antibodies are produced, this person is able to infect others.) Once antibodies have been produced, they will show up on a blood test called the HIV antibody test. The presence of antibodies is a sign that the person is infected and therefore able to infect others. However, he or she may continue to look and feel healthy for a long time after infection occurs. If the immune system is already weak, AIDS-related symptoms may show up more quickly. Factors that can speed up the development of symptoms include stress, not enough sleep, poor nutrition, drug abuse, and other infections.

Strangely enough, HIV itself does not actually kill the people it infects. Rather, people with AIDS die from other infections that are able to do great harm because the body can no longer protect itself. These infections are called opportunistic infections. They were so named because they take the opportunity to attack when the immune system is weak.

AIDS-related diseases tend to have long, strange-sounding names, such as cryptosporidiosis. Ten years ago, most people had never heard of many of these diseases. The germs that cause these illnesses are really not that rare in our society. However, it is unusual for people with healthy immune systems to be made sick by them. Healthy bodies are able to successfully keep these microorganisms under control.

Before developing AIDS, most infected people first come down with a milder illness called AIDS-Related Complex (ARC or HIV-related illness).

## AIDS-Related Complex (ARC)

The symptoms of AIDS-Related Complex (ARC) are like those produced by other less serious illnesses, such as a bad case of flu. However, a person with ARC will also show signs of HIV infection when a blood sample is taken. ARC symptoms, which often persist for months at a time, include:

- Severe fatigue
- Swollen glands (lymph nodes) in the neck, groin, and armpits
- Fevers (101-102 degrees)
- Chills; night sweats
- Loss of appetite
- A weight loss of more than ten pounds for no apparent reason
- Diarrhea

For every one case of AIDS reported, at least ten cases of ARC are diagnosed. A person with ARC may be sick for months or even years before progressing to full-blown AIDS. Some ARC patients become so severely ill, they die without ever developing AIDS. Anyone who has ARC symptoms for more than two weeks should see a doctor.

## AIDS

A person is not considered to have full-blown AIDS until he or she has been diagnosed with a specific infection or cancer associated with severe HIV infection. The two most common such diseases are pneumocystis carinii pneumonia, a serious lung infection, and Kaposi's sarcoma, a kind of skin cancer. About 85 percent of AIDS

*The dark blotches of Kaposi's sarcoma are evident in this picture of a patient's heel. Kaposi's sarcoma, or KS, occurs in about 30 percent of AIDS patients.*

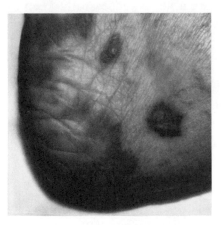

patients have one or both of these diseases. Because these two opportunistic diseases are normally very rare, they are considered markers for full-blown AIDS.

Diarrhea, swollen glands, and other ARC symptoms are all common in AIDS patients. People with AIDS may also experience shortness of breath, trouble breathing, white patches in the mouth, and skin rashes. The opportunistic infections they suffer are often severe enough to require staying in a hospital. Some AIDS patients develop a progressive brain disorder called AIDS dementia complex. In patients with this disorder, the brain tissue and spinal column slowly deteriorate. Symptoms include headaches, forgetfulness, an inability to concentrate, memory loss, and weakness in the arms and legs. This condition, however, is not as common as the following two diseases, which result in a substantial number of AIDS deaths.

## Pneumocystis carinii pneumonia (PCP)

About 75 percent of all AIDS patients get a rare lung disease called pneumocystis carinii pneumonia (PCP) at least once during their illness. Second and third bouts of PCP are generally harder to treat than the first. Often the patient does not survive. Symptoms include

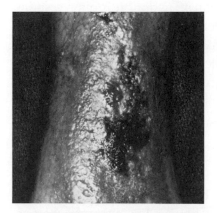

*Kaposi's sarcoma badly discolors this patient's ankle. Usually a rarely found, superficial skin cancer, KS can ravage every organ in an AIDS victim's body.*

fever, a persistent dry cough, and trouble breathing. PCP is the leading cause of death among AIDS patients.

## Kaposi's sarcoma (KS)

Kaposi's sarcoma (KS) is a rare kind of cancer characterized by purplish-brown spots on or under the skin. The bruise-like blotches may be either flat or raised. They most often occur on the upper body, neck, and face. About 30 percent of all AIDS patients suffer from KS. Before the AIDS epidemic, KS was mainly a disease of elderly men of East European descent. Within this group, it is not a very serious disease and usually affects only the skin. In AIDS patients, however, the cancerous masses have been known to spread to almost every organ of the body. The infection is particularly severe if it involves the lungs.

Another unusual infection often seen in people with AIDS is mycobacterium avium-intracellulare (MAI), a lung disease like tuberculosis. This disease afflicts about 50 percent of AIDS patients. It causes severe breathing problems and may also spread to the digestive system, spleen, and liver. The disease progresses quickly. Its survival rate is poor if the patient does not receive treatment.

Persistent diarrhea is another common affliction. It is often responsible for the severe weight loss experienced by many people with AIDS. Some of these AIDS-related intestinal infections are extremely uncommon in humans. For example, cryptosporidiosis is a life-threatening kind of diarrhea that normally afflicts birds, fish, reptiles, and mammals. Before 1981, only seven persons in the world had been diagnosed with this disease. Now it is frequently seen in people with AIDS.

Some AIDS-related infections are caused by ordinary "bugs" that may have been in the patient's body for years without causing harm. It is only when the immune system becomes weakened that these "bugs" are able to cause serious problems. For example, herpes simplex, the virus responsible for cold sores and fever blisters, is present in the bodies of most people. Much of the time, this virus is inactive and may not cause symptoms for years at a time. However, when a person with herpes gets extremely tired or is under severe stress, the virus may flare up. When this happens, one or more cold sores or fever blisters generally show up on the person's lip or inside the mouth. In AIDS patients, however, herpes infections are more serious and can involve other parts of the body. Besides numerous blisters, the virus can cause an infection of the lungs and even a brain disease called encephalitis.

Several HIV-related infections are caused by microorganisms called fungi. The most common fungal infection—oral candida or thrush—causes white patches in the mouth and a coating on the tongue. Thrush is annoying and sometimes quite painful. But it rarely spreads beyond the mouth and throat. Infections caused by some kinds of fungi, on the other hand, can involve the lungs, brain, and other vital organs.

## Can people survive with AIDS?

Because they are subject to so many life-threatening infections, most AIDS patients die within three years of being diagnosed with the disease. Yet somehow thousands of people, about 15 percent of all AIDS patients, have been able to beat these odds. Those who have had AIDS for three years or longer are called "long-term survivors." Most are active and seem to be in good health. They are not cured of AIDS, but they have learned to live with it.

How have they done this? Some experts think they may be naturally more resistant to HIV. Perhaps their immune systems are stronger. Others attribute long-term survival to certain personality characteristics. A positive outlook, the ability to talk openly about their illness, and a strong sense of purpose may help AIDS patients live longer. It is common for long-term survivors to have a good sense of humor and to love life. And many are actively involved in helping other AIDS patients.

## The HIV antibody test

In 1985, a blood test to detect infection with HIV became available. It was first developed to screen donated blood to make sure the blood supply was safe. Now this test is available to let concerned persons know if they have been exposed to HIV. It does not show the presence of the virus, but rather the antibodies produced by the body to destroy the virus. The presence of antibodies in the blood means HIV has entered the body and the immune system is reacting to it. Certain groups of people are considered at high risk for infection with HIV. Persons in the high-risk groups listed below may want to get an HIV antibody test:

- Homosexual and bisexual men
- People who use or have used IV drugs, especially if they have shared needles
- People who received transfusions of donated blood or blood products between 1977 and March 1985
- Prostitutes (men and women) and others who have had many sexual partners

- People who have had sex with someone who has AIDS or someone who is known to be infected with HIV
- People who have had sex (even once) since 1977 with a partner in one or more of the above groups

Anyone who is sexually active, especially if he or she has had more than one partner, may want to take the test.

Many public health agencies give free HIV antibody testing. (Information on places that perform testing is available through local health departments and the American Red Cross.) It is possible in many places for a person to be tested without having to give his or her name. Instead, an identification number is assigned and this number is attached to the person's blood sample. Thus, test results are confidential. Testing can also be done for a small charge in a doctor's office or at a private medical lab. Results of tests done under these conditions, however, will become a part of the person's medical record.

## Testing procedures

Testing procedures are different from community to community. The process described here is typical of that used in many public health agencies. The process generally begins with an interview with a trained counselor. The counselor talks about high-risk behaviors and the meaning of test results with the person to be tested. Following the counseling session, a small sample of blood is taken and is labeled with an identification number. The person is given a slip of paper with the ID number and is told when to return for test results.

One very reliable test used to detect HIV antibodies is the EIA (enzyme immunoassay). If a blood sample shows the presence of HIV antibodies, the test is said to be positive. To make certain a mistake has not been made, positive tests are usually rechecked at least once more. (It is possible, but rare, to have a blood sample test positive without actually being infected. When this happens, it is called a ''false positive.'') A different test called the Western Blot is often used to confirm a positive EIA. After all tests are finished the person being tested returns to the agency for a second appointment. The person presents his or her identification number and meets with a trained counselor to get test results.

A negative test result means no measurable antibodies were in the person's blood *at the time the blood sample was taken*. Does this mean the person is free from infection? Not always. If the person did not participate in high-risk behaviors during the six months before the test, the test result is probably quite accurate. However, under other circumstances, a person might test negative even though he or she is actually infected. (This is called a "false negative.") Infection

*Medical researcher Francis Chandler uses an electron microscope to study and photograph viruses. Viruses are too small—many times smaller than bacteria—to be seen through a common, lighted microscope.*

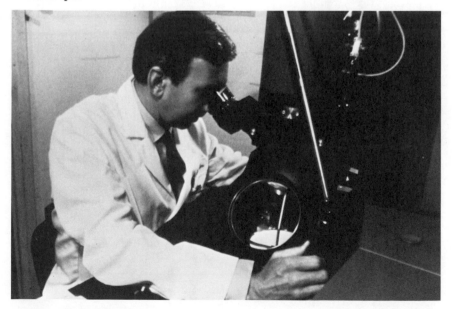

may have taken place several weeks before the test, but the immune system may not yet have made antibodies. ''False negatives'' are most likely to occur in people who repeatedly practice high-risk behaviors, such as sharing IV needles or having anal intercourse. Infection can occur at any time under these conditions. Therefore, for these people, a single negative test cannot be relied upon. Accurate results require that a person refrain from high-risk activities for six months before being tested (or retested).

## A positive test

*A positive test does not mean a person has AIDS.* It does mean the person is a carrier of the virus and will be for the rest of his or her life. The infected person should inform current and past sexual partners about the positive test result and suggest that they may

'... Getting married ?!... No, we're just considering dating...'

also want to be tested. To prevent infecting others with HIV, persons who test positive should also take the following precautions:

- Do not allow others to use personal hygiene items that might be contaminated with blood (razors, toothbrushes, and others). Needles used to inject drugs, legal or otherwise, *should never be shared.*
- Abstain from sex or practice only protected sex
- Avoid pregnancy
- Do not donate blood, organs, or sperm

People who test positive need not feel helpless and hopeless. The first thing such people should do is see a doctor for a complete medical checkup and evaluation. There are a number of things that can be done to protect and prolong good health. Good health habits are particularly important for those infected with HIV. These habits include eating nutritious meals, getting plenty of rest, and exercising regularly. Thinking positively and learning ways to cope with stress will also help. Because the AIDS virus is not spread through casual contact, special precautions at school, work, or in social situations are not necessary.

CHAPTER THREE

# AIDS: A Personal Tragedy

In the first few years of the AIDS epidemic, most Americans paid little attention to the disease. Some didn't even know it existed. Others were only mildly curious about the strange new affliction. During these years, thousands of people around the country became sick and died. Friends and families grieved, but few others took notice.

Then something happened that put the disease on the front pages of America's newspapers. Rock Hudson, a famous movie star, became ill with AIDS. In August 1985, newspaper articles described Hudson's weakened state and his sudden trip to France for treatment. Within a few months, the popular actor was dead.

Hudson's death shocked the world. For millions, AIDS was now a reality. It finally had a face they recognized. People began to pay more attention to the disease and to those it affected.

Shortly before he died, Hudson asked that this statement be read at a fundraiser for AIDS: "I am not happy that I am sick. I am not happy that I have AIDS. But if that is helping others, I can at least know that my own misfortune has had some positive worth."

Those who are not infected have responded to the AIDS epidemic in different ways. The truth is that this major health crisis has brought out the best and worst in people.

On the negative side, many people with AIDS have been the victims of discrimination. They have been called names, spit upon, and even shot at. They have been refused medical and dental care, been fired from their jobs, evicted from their homes, and sometimes rejected by friends and family. Children with AIDS often have been barred from attending school. Even in death, people with AIDS have been discriminated against. Some funeral homes have refused to prepare their bodies for burial. It is no wonder that AIDS is called a lonely disease.

But there has also been much compassion. Thousands have responded to this national catastrophe by offering love and support to people with AIDS. Volunteers have helped AIDS patients in many ways. They have cleaned their homes, prepared their meals, and provided them with transportation. They have helped them get the financial assistance and medical care they need. They have held them close when others were afraid to come near.

What is it like to suffer from AIDS? What is it like to be the friend or relative of someone who is dying from the disease? The following story tells of one young AIDS patient and his family.

## David Mandell

David Mandell was a normal fifth-grader in many ways. He liked astronauts, computers, the television star Alf, hamburgers, flashy sports cars, and life in general. David was a happy kid. He was also a hemophiliac.

David started receiving Factor VIII for his hemophilia when he was two years old. Although neither he nor his family knew it, by the time he was eight, he had become infected with HIV. The virus soon spread throughout his system. When David was ten, he was diagnosed with AIDS.

The first sign of David's illness was a lump on his neck. Doctors did tests and discovered David had non-Hodgkins lymphoma, a kind of cancer that was just beginning to be associated with AIDS. David was tested for HIV antibodies and found to be infected.

The lump on David's neck grew until it was the size of a grapefruit.

*David Mandell, a young hemophiliac, died of AIDS after receiving an HIV-infected blood transfusion. Before a blood-screening technique was invented, many hemophiliacs received HIV-infected blood and later developed AIDS.*

In an attempt to kill the lymphoma, David's doctors used four experimental kinds of chemotherapy. The strong anticancer drugs used in the treatments made David sick to his stomach and caused his hair and eyelashes to fall out. The drugs also affected his body's ability to make new blood cells, and he had to have many blood tests. David's father went to the hospital often to donate blood for his son.

Friends knew David had cancer, but they didn't know he had AIDS. David's parents didn't tell very many people. They wanted their son to lead a normal life as long as possible. They didn't worry about David infecting his friends because they knew AIDS is not spread through casual contact.

David and his mother called AIDS "the beastie," because it was like a monster that had sneaked into his body. Life with "the beastie" was painful, but David was courageous. He was cheerful most of the time and did not want pity or sympathy. He just wanted to be treated like a normal kid.

David didn't worry about himself as much as he worried about those around him. As his symptoms got worse, David became afraid to play with his friends. He thought he might make them sick. He even worried about making his doctor sick. His parents told him this wouldn't happen. But David still had nightmares about it.

Three months before he died, David turned eleven. For a birthday celebration, a family friend took David out to a fancy restaurant. The friend wore a tuxedo. So did David. A limousine took them to the restaurant where they dined on stuffed crab and fresh strawberries. David was very happy that night. He loved limousines, and strawberries were his favorite food.

David was in and out of the hospital many times during the last few months of his life. He lost weight, dropping from seventy-five to fifty-three pounds. He suffered from many infections, including a fungal infection in his throat. This made it terribly painful to swallow. His kidneys began to fail and his body swelled up. On January 21, 1988, David died.

Several weeks later, David's schoolmates held a balloon launch in memory of their friend. They released hundreds of balloons from the school playground. Each balloon had a photo of David attached to it. On the back of the photo was this message: "He lived, loved, and was loved. Now he has gone to his highest expectation."

A very good thing happened after David's death. David's parents started going to meetings and conferences to tell others about AIDS. They wanted people of all ages to know more about the deadly disease that can strike anyone. They also wanted to reach out to others who were struggling with "the beastie." Even David's teenage sister started going out to schools to speak to other young people about AIDS.

David Mandell died within a year of being diagnosed with AIDS. Other patients, for reasons unknown, have lived for five years or more after developing their first symptoms. One such person is Rick Anderson.

## Rick Anderson

"I want to squeeze every moment out of life," says Rick, a thirty-one-year-old homosexual man. But Rick can't squeeze very hard these days. A ten-year struggle with HIV has sapped him of much of his energy.

"I used to run, play tennis, and stay up late," says Rick. "Now I'm limited. It makes me angry that I can't be a fully functioning person anymore." Rick believes he was infected with HIV about ten years ago through a homosexual relationship with a man who has since died of AIDS. Rick's body has been further weakened by a liver disease and an inflammation of the lining of the brain.

His first clue that anything was wrong came in 1981, the year the first AIDS cases were diagnosed. Rick went to a doctor because his tongue was sore and had white blotches on it. His condition was

*AIDS patient Rick Anderson (center) participates in a 1987 march commemorating those who died of AIDS in San Diego County, California. Rick is a long-term survivor of the inevitably fatal disease.*

diagnosed as oral candida (thrush). But the doctor had no idea what was causing it. Rick thought it might be a result of smoking too much, so he gave up cigarettes. The symptoms persisted, however, and, as time went on, new ones appeared. In 1984, suffering from constant fatigue, he went in for another checkup. This time, the doctor detected swollen lymph glands in Rick's neck, underarms, and groin. The diagnosis was AIDS-Related Complex (or Pre-AIDS as it was called at that time).

## Dealing with his own death

Rick was only twenty-five when he learned what was wrong with him. He says dealing with the possibility of an early death was the hardest thing he ever went through. His first reaction was anger, but that was quickly followed by a determination to get his health back. He started by learning everything he could about the human body, nutrition, and AIDS. He ate healthy foods and took many vitamins. For a while he even traveled to Mexico to buy drugs he couldn't get in the United States. Before long, his efforts paid off. His thrush cleared up and he began to have more energy.

But HIV infection is marked by setbacks, ups and downs, and changes in patterns. By late 1984, his symptoms were back. This time they were so severe he had to quit his job. By 1985, the virus had begun to affect Rick's brain, causing concentration problems and some memory loss. Going back to work was no longer a possibility. Because he was disabled, Rick began to receive a small amount of money from the federal government each month.

Despite the pain, frustration, and uncertainty that each day brings, Rick tries to maintain a positive mental attitude. He eats nutritiously and takes several medications his doctor has prescribed. He is hopeful that a cure for AIDS will be found in time to help him. "There's a distinct possibility I could live forever," he says. "But there's also a distinct possibility I could die next year."

Rick presently serves as a member of his community's task force

on AIDS. He feels strongly about warning people about the danger of HIV infection. "More Americans have died from AIDS than died in the Vietnam War," he says. He also believes people need to be reassured that AIDS is not spread through casual contact. Rick knows such contact is not a danger through his own experience with family members. When his sister was going through a divorce in 1985, Rick's three young nieces came to live with him. The girls were five, six, and seven when they moved in. Although Rick and the girls used separate bathrooms, there were no other special living arrangements. Affection was openly shown, with hugs and kisses every day. But just to be sure, "I didn't kiss them on the lips," says Rick.

## Playing nurse to uncle

Most days Rick had enough energy to prepare meals for the children and to get them to and from school. But there were also times when the girls took care of him. "They would fight over who got my medicine for me," he says. "They really liked playing nurse." The girls tried to be quiet when Rick was napping, but they weren't always successful. Once, one of the young "nurses" prepared a full breakfast for him and brought it to his bedside. Rick would have enjoyed it more had she picked a better time—it was four o'clock in the morning!

Rick, who is now back to living alone, spends a lot of his time thinking these days. He doesn't know what his future will bring. But he does know that many good things have come from his illness. The experience has helped him to better understand life and to learn more about who he is. "I'm not afraid to die anymore," he says. "That's okay now."

David Mandell and Rick Anderson are just two of over thousands of Americans who have been stricken with AIDS since 1981. The disease has many other faces. AIDS is also:

- The young mother of six who became infected through sexual intercourse with her husband, an IV drug user.
- The seventy-year-old man who died of AIDS five years after receiving contaminated blood during heart surgery.
- The six-month-old baby with AIDS who is well enough to leave the hospital, but who has no one to care for him.
- The doctor who diagnosed himself with AIDS after discovering the lesions of Kaposi's sarcoma on his body.

Others affected by AIDS include those left behind when a loved one dies of the disease. Some family members and friends are devastated by the experience. Others find positive ways to work through their grief. The NAMES Project has helped many to do this.

## The NAMES Project

The NAMES Project National AIDS Memorial Quilt has been called the "largest community arts project in the country." It is a national memorial to men, women, and children who have died from AIDS in the United States. But, the quilt does more than memorialize those who have died from AIDS. It also shows the size of the epidemic and its tragic cost in human lives.

The National AIDS Memorial Quilt is made up of thousands of six-by-three-foot panels. Each panel represents a person who has died from the disease. Eight panels are sewn together to make one quilt section. There are hundreds of sections, and the quilt is still growing.

Cleve Jones of San Francisco had the idea for the project. He saw a quilt as the perfect symbol of compassion for those who have suffered and died from AIDS. He thought this because quilts provide warmth and are often associated with comforting the sick. Each panel of the quilt was made by a family member or friend of a person who died from AIDS. Cleve Jones calls the quilt "a statement of hope and remembrance, a symbol of national unity, and a promise of love."

Much creativity is shown in the design of the panels. Materials used include leather, silk, shower curtains, jeans, flags, bed sheets, and carpet. Objects that remind friends of the loved one are often attached to a panel. These reminders include stuffed animals, T-shirts, photographs, artificial flowers, sequins, balloons, Vietnam War medals, and seashells.

The quilt was first displayed in October 1987 in Washington, D.C. At that time it had over two thousand panels. When it was unfolded in the park between the Washington Monument and the U.S. Capitol Building, it covered three-fourths of this grassy area.

*This photograph of the NAMES Project National AIDS Memorial Quilt was taken from the top of the Washington monument as the quilt was spread out on the Ellipse in Washington, D.C. The quilt is made up of individual, unique panels, each commemorating a person who has died of AIDS.*

*Movie idol Rock Hudson's losing battle with AIDS brought the disease to America's attention in 1985. Since his death, many Hollywood celebrities have actively campaigned in the fight against AIDS.*

In 1988, the quilt took a four-month, twelve-thousand-mile tour around the United States. It was displayed in twenty cities in all parts of the country. In October 1988, it returned to the nation's capital for a national day of remembrance. The quilt by then contained 8,288 panels. When spread out, it covered an area the size of eight football fields!

The quilt has a panel for David Mandell, the young hemophiliac whose story was told earlier in this chapter. The quilt also has one in memory of Rock Hudson. The two pieces of material are exactly the same size.

As has been shown, AIDS affects not only the patient, but all who come in contact with him or her. Family members, friends, co-workers, even casual acquaintances are all affected. Those close to the patient can help by offering love and support. They can also help by educating others about what AIDS is and is not.

## Activists for AIDS

An activist is someone who takes vigorous action in support of a cause. Many activists for AIDS have participated in parades and

*In October 1987, thousands of people with AIDS and their supporters marched in Washington, D.C. They were protesting that the government was not doing enough to fight the spread of AIDS or to help AIDS patients.*

demonstrations across the nation to call attention to the problems caused by the AIDS epidemic. For example, in October 1988, over one thousand people took part in a demonstration at the Food and Drug Administration building in Washington, D.C. They were protesting the government's slowness in making drugs available for the treatment of AIDS. Earlier in the year, several thousand people had marched in Sacramento, California, to call attention to the need for increased funding for AIDS programs and research. A third group of activists trespassed at the headquarters of an Illinois drug manufacturer. They were protesting a huge price increase for a drug used to treat AIDS-related pneumonia.

Many communities hold annual walkathons to raise money for AIDS programs and agencies. Usually participants walk a certain distance and their sponsors then pay a specified amount for each kilometer or mile walked. In one such event, about ten thousand walkers raised 1.5 million dollars for the Los Angeles AIDS Project.

Activists include people of all ages and races. Even children take part in events such as walkathons. Most activists are ordinary people whose names are not well known. But some activists are famous. For example, many stars from the entertainment world have raised money to help people with AIDS and to fund research. Celebrity activists include actresses Elizabeth Taylor and Patty Duke, singers Dionne Warwick and Elton John, and comedienne Joan Rivers. Elizabeth Taylor is National Chairman of the American Foundation for AIDS Research (AmFAR), a nonprofit organization that raises money for AIDS research.

Many authors and playwrights have drawn attention to AIDS by using it as a theme in their writings. In 1985, the play *As Is* won a New York drama award. In that same year, a television production called *An Early Frost* was awarded an Emmy. Episodes about AIDS have appeared on several television series, including "L.A. Law," "Cagney and Lacey," "St. Elsewhere," and "Designing Women."

CHAPTER FOUR

# AIDS Prevention

The best way to prevent AIDS is to teach people how the disease is spread and to encourage them to avoid high-risk activities. The earliest attempts to provide this kind of information were made by members of the gay (homosexual) community. Because of these early educational efforts, many gay and bisexual men have changed their behaviors. Today many remain free of HIV infection.

As the AIDS epidemic spread, it became obvious that additional educational efforts were needed. Federal, state and local health agencies provided information to school districts, hospitals, law enforcement agencies, businesses, community organizations, and many other groups.

The major agency involved in AIDS education is the U.S. Public Health Service (USPHS). This agency is headed by the Surgeon General of the United States. (The Centers for Disease Control in Atlanta is a part of this governmental agency.) In 1986, former Surgeon General C. Everett Koop issued his *Report on Acquired Immune Deficiency Syndrome*, which stressed the importance of AIDS education.

In the spring of 1988, the United States government launched a national campaign to reach all citizens with information about AIDS. A pamphlet on AIDS was prepared and sent to every household in the country. The mailing included 110 million pamphlets in English and 4 million in Spanish.

Information on AIDS is available from a variety of other sources, including libraries, the American Red Cross, local public health agencies, and AIDS organizations.

## AIDS education in school

AIDS education at an early age is critical if the killer disease is to be conquered. Fortunately, most Americans support the teaching of such information in school. (In one poll, 83 percent of those questioned backed such programs.) Today, many of the country's school districts provide AIDS education. The Surgeon General recommends that AIDS education start no later than middle school (Grades 6-8).

About 1 percent of those diagnosed with AIDS in the U.S. are teenagers. A much larger number (21 percent) are between twenty and twenty-nine years old. It must be remembered, however, that HIV has a long incubation period, sometimes seven years or more. So it is possible that many AIDS patients now in their twenties became infected while in their teens. This is why it is particularly important that young people learn about AIDS and how it is transmitted *before* they become sexually active and before they are tempted to experiment with IV drugs.

AIDS is a preventable disease. If people can prevent HIV from entering their bodies, they will never get AIDS. There are only a few ways the virus can get inside the body. The most common way is through sex.

## Sex and AIDS

In today's world, sex can indeed be a life-threatening activity. But it need not be for people who take the time to learn ways to protect themselves. The best protection against sexually transmitted HIV is abstinence. Abstinence means not having sex at all. For young people, this is the recommended way to protect oneself. Abstinence also eliminates the possibility of unplanned pregnancy and offers protection against other sexually transmitted diseases. Such diseases are dangerous because they often cause sores that provide an easy way for HIV to enter the body.

Each person is responsible for his or her own sexual behavior. No one should ever feel pressured into sexual intercourse or other risky behaviors. It is perfectly okay to say "no" to sex. There are many ways to express sexual feelings without having sexual intercourse. These include touching, hugging, caressing, and massaging. These are all healthy, safe, and enjoyable ways to give and receive affection.

The safest kind of sexual relationship is a monogamous one (two people having sex only with each other). But partners must be able to trust each other. Knowing the sexual history of one's partner and being able to trust him or her is a matter of life and death in today's world. Anyone who cannot be absolutely sure a partner is free from

*Larina Williams (left) and Jeanette Stoney (right) of Palo Alto, California, watch Andy Answer in the video called "A Is for AIDS" in which both girls starred. The video educates children about AIDS.*

infection should either abstain from sex or have only protected sex.

Protected sex involves using a condom, a rubber sheath that fits over a man's penis. The condom traps semen released from the penis. This prevents the semen from entering the woman's vagina. It also offers protection to the man by providing a barrier against vaginal secretions. No condom is 100 percent safe, however. During the motion of intercourse, the condom can break or slip off, making infection possible. Some condoms may even have tiny holes in them. It is also very important that the condom be used throughout the entire sex act. This means it should be put on before intercourse is attempted. It should be left on until semen is released and the man withdraws his penis.

Condoms are available in drug stores and can be purchased by both men and women. No one should be embarrassed to buy such protection. Condoms made of latex are the best kind to use because HIV cannot pass through this material.

*Beverlie Conant Sloane, a health educator at Dartmouth College in New Hampshire, holds one of the condom kits given out to students at the Dartmouth Health Center. The kits are meant to promote safe sex on campus.*

# AIDS HAS NO SEXUAL PREFERENCE.

If you still think AIDS only affects homosexuals, you're wrong, and you could be dead wrong. Anyone, gay or straight, male or female, can get AIDS.

People infected with the AIDS virus may not look sick. So practice responsible sex. Start by talking to your partner about AIDS. Make smart choices. You can say no or stick with one partner.

If you have more than one partner, always use condoms and spermicides.

Want to know more about AIDS, the right way to use a condom, or how to educate your children about AIDS? Call the Minnesota AIDSLine at 1-800-248-AIDS for immediate, accurate, private and personalized information.

## Anyone Can Get AIDS. Everyone Can Prevent It.

Drug abuse plays a key role in the spread of AIDS because persons who are addicted to drugs do not often stop to take precautions. Drug users frequently share needles. They are also more likely to have unprotected sex. These high-risk activities jeopardize their lives, and the lives of others.

Some addicts inject drugs in "shooting galleries." These are secluded places like alleys and abandoned buildings where many people share a few needles. People who frequent such places are at high risk of becoming infected with HIV. As with sex, abstinence is the best way to avoid the possibility of HIV infection. The best preventive measure is to simply say "no" to drugs.

Efforts have been made to inform IV drug users about the risk of HIV infection and to encourage them to seek treatment for their drug addiction. Most communities have organizations and clinics that can provide assistance. Drug users can also call the National Institute of Drug Abuse Hotline for help (1-800-662-HELP).

*Outside city health department offices, supporters of a New York City AIDS-prevention program warn people of the dangers of sharing needles. The program provides free needles to drug addicts in the hope of slowing the spread of AIDS. Sharing dirty needles is a major cause of AIDS infection.*

Many drug users, however, cannot or are unwilling to give up their habits. Helping these people involves teaching them to keep their drug equipment (works) clean and warning them about the hazards of sharing their needles. Drug equipment can easily be sterilized by using bleach, rubbing alcohol, or boiling water.

Many people who shoot drugs are already infected with HIV. For example, it is estimated that about half of the IV drug users in New York City have HIV in their bodies. To combat further spread of the virus, several cities have started needle exchange programs. These are programs where any IV drug user can bring in a used needle and get a clean one for free. Other cities provide bleach to IV drug users so they can disinfect their equipment.

## Other risk areas

Several groups of workers need to be particularly cautious because of the kind of work they do. One of these groups is health-care workers. This group includes doctors, nurses, and medical lab employees. These people need to protect themselves because they may be exposed to infected body fluids while working with patients.

There are over six million health-care workers in the United States. As of 1988, fewer than twenty of them had been reported as having been infected with HIV through their work. Usually the workers were infected as a result of being pricked accidentally with an HIV-contaminated needle.

Most health-care workers are very careful when handling needles and other sharp instruments. They also wear protective clothing (rubber gloves and gowns) to prevent direct contact with infected body fluids. They are taught to dispose of contaminated items promptly to avoid exposing others to HIV.

It is now common practice for dentists and dental assistants to wear gloves and face protection (mask and protective eyewear) while performing dental procedures. This offers protection to both patient and dental worker against transmittal of HIV.

*Designer Larry Kangas is shown modeling Tough Gloves. Kangas developed the metal-mesh gloves to protect surgeons and other medical personnel who may cut themselves while working. The gloves prevent health care workers from coming in contact with AIDS-infected blood or other fluids.*

Other workers who might accidentally be exposed to HIV infection include police officers, fire fighters, and emergency medical technicians. Such workers frequently come in contact with persons who are bleeding. Therefore, guidelines to prevent possible infection have been set up in a number of cities.

CHAPTER FIVE

# Help for the AIDS Patient

No drug available today can cure AIDS. Scientists do not know if a cure ever will be found. Although progress has been made in controlling HIV, it may not be possible to rid the body of the virus once infection has occurred. Treatments are available, however, that can both prolong and ease the lives of AIDS patients. Some treatments also show promise for use with healthy persons who are HIV positive. Early use of some drugs may help these people maintain their health.

## Medical treatments

The Food and Drug Administration (FDA) is an agency of the U.S. Public Health Service. One of its jobs is to approve new drugs proposed for the treatment of various diseases. AZT (azidothymidine or zidovudine) is the only drug that the FDA has approved for the treatment of AIDS. AZT does not cure AIDS, but the drug is able to slow down the course of the disease. It does this by interfering with HIV's ability to reproduce within the host cell.

AZT, now used by thousands, first became available in March 1987. It got widespread use under a one-year, thirty-million-dollar government program that began in September 1987. This program provided the drug at no cost to many AIDS patients across the country. Because it is very expensive (about eight thousand dollars a year per patient), few people with AIDS would be able to purchase AZT on their own.

Although it has improved the life of many people with AIDS, AZT does have some drawbacks. It is a toxic drug and can cause side effects, such as nausea, rashes, and headaches. AZT can also suppress bone marrow, the part of the body that makes blood cells. Sometimes the ability to produce new blood cells is so impaired that blood transfusions are needed. Most AIDS patients, however, are willing to put up with these side effects in order to live a longer life.

The benefits of AZT were shown in a study done with two groups of AIDS patients. All of them had had pneumocystis carinii pneumonia (PCP). During the study, half of the patients took AZT for a year. At the end of the year, almost three-quarters of the patients that took AZT were still alive. In the group that did not take the drug, only half had survived.

Studies are also being done on the effects of AZT on people who have tested positive for HIV but who do not yet have symptoms. It is hoped that early treatment will delay or prevent the development of HIV-related disease in these carriers. And since the people are in good health, they should experience fewer side effects. AZT tests are also being done with health workers who have accidentally been exposed to infected blood and other body fluids. Perhaps by taking AZT for six weeks after exposure, infection can be prevented. A third group that might benefit from the drug is infected women who are pregnant. AZT may be able to prevent the transmission of HIV from these mothers to their unborn children.

## Experimental drugs

Although AZT is the only drug approved for AIDS treatment, other drugs are being studied on a trial basis with small groups of volunteers. Many AIDS patients volunteer for these experimental programs, but the number that can participate is limited. The effect of these drugs on humans generally is not known. Therefore, volunteers are warned that some risks are involved.

It takes an average of eight years for the FDA to evaluate and approve a new drug. This length of time is needed to find out if the drug is safe for people to use. The FDA decides this after laboratory research and many tests on animals and humans. For AIDS patients, however, eight years is much too long to wait for help. They would be dead by the time the drug was approved. In the case of AZT, the government sped up its usually lengthy approval process. It was released for use in less than three years.

In July 1988, the FDA also began allowing patients to import drugs that are not legal to treat AIDS in the United States. The drugs are not legal in this country because the FDA has not yet studied them. AIDS patients may use the drugs to treat their own illness, but are not allowed to sell them. Before the FDA ruling, a number of patients had purchased the drugs illegally. Some imported them from other countries. Others obtained them from illegal drug laboratories in the United States called guerrilla labs. Even if the drugs did not

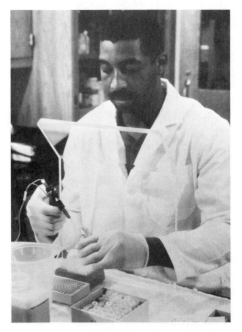

*Researcher Larry Wells performs a standard test for the presence of HIV in laboratory blood samples. A "positive" result means that antibodies for HIV were found in the blood.*

help, the patients felt they had nothing to lose. They were going to die of AIDS anyway.

Dextran sulfate is among the dozens of experimental drugs now being studied for the treatment of AIDS. It has been used as a blood-thinning drug in Japan for twenty years. Some researchers believe that dextran sulfate may be able to interfere with HIV's ability to attach itself to blood cells. Since it is not yet available in the United States, some AIDS patients import this drug from Japan and Mexico.

Many lives are also being prolonged by the successful treatment of severe opportunistic infections, particularly PCP. Trimetrexate and pentamidine are two FDA-approved drugs that effectively treat this disease. Several treatments that can actually *prevent* PCP are now being hailed as valuable weapons against AIDS. An inhaled kind of pentamidine and a drug combination (sulfamethoxazole and trimethoprim) can prolong lives by protecting people with AIDS from the ravages of PCP. PCP is the leading cause of death in people with AIDS.

## Nutritional supplements

Many nutritional supplements believed to be helpful in combatting AIDS are available at health food stores and pharmacies. Others are available through buyers clubs (groups of patients and friends working together to obtain special products in large quantities).

AL-721 is a substance made from eggs and soybeans. It is the supplement most widely used by AIDS patients (about 15,000). Some researchers believe AL-721 may be able to interfere with HIV's ability to pass into cells. AL-721 softens cell walls. The researchers think the softened walls may be more difficult for the virus to attach to. Other widely used supplements are herbs, aloe vera juice, garlic, flower pollen, vitamins A, C, and E, and the minerals selenium and zinc.

Although effective medical treatments are important, AIDS patients have other critical needs. These include emotional support, financial assistance, and help with daily life problems. Possibly the most important need of people with AIDS is that of love and support. AIDS patients not only suffer the physical pain of their illness, but also the emotional pain of dealing with a terminal disease. Facing death is difficult at any age, but it is overwhelming to those who are young and in their most productive years. Fear and anger are often the first reactions to an AIDS diagnosis.

Guilt, self-blame, and depression are also common emotions in AIDS patients. The patient may feel guilty for the behavior that brought about the disease—IV drug use, promiscuity (having sex with many partners), risky sexual activity. Friends and family can help by communicating their acceptance and concern for the patient. This is important because feelings of rejection, helplessness, and anxiety can further suppress an already weakened immune system. Fortunately, help in dealing with these emotions is available from many AIDS support groups. There are hundreds of such groups across the country. Most telephone directories list local organizations.

## Support groups

Special support groups help AIDS and ARC patients learn to deal with their illness by offering counseling and therapy. This is often accomplished in discussion groups where patients can share their feelings and give and get emotional support. Individual counseling and family sessions are also generally available. Many support groups extend their programs to include persons who have tested HIV-positive and are concerned about maintaining their health.

Other services typically provided by support groups include assistance with basic needs (housing, food, and clothing), recreational programs, and legal advice. Some organizations have extensive educational programs, with lending libraries, telephone hot-lines, and speakers bureaus. A few support groups focus on helping the patient adopt and maintain a positive attitude since hope and a positive outlook are known to be beneficial to the immune system.

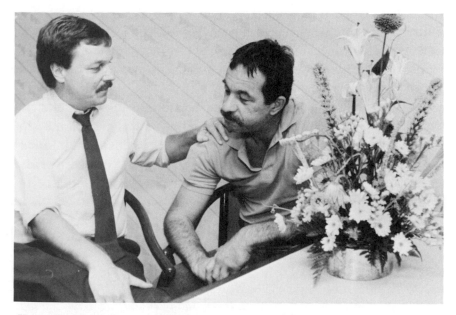

*Kevin Burke (left), an AIDS worker in a California care center, consoles Stanley Vitalone whose lover is dying of AIDS. AIDS workers are a new group of medical personnel trained to help people cope with AIDS.*

Many groups provide what is known as a "buddy" program. This program matches a patient with AIDS with a healthy volunteer (buddy). In the later stages of the disease, people with AIDS need help with everyday activities, such as going to the store, cooking, and cleaning the house. Buddies can help in all these areas.

One of the largest, and oldest, support groups in the country is the Gay Men's Health Crisis (GMHC) in New York City. GMHC has over one thousand volunteers who help with the organization's many service programs. San Francisco, a city with thousands of AIDS patients, has over one hundred nonprofit AIDS support groups. They offer just about every service an AIDS patient might need or want.

There is even a special program called PAWS (Pets Are Wonderful Support) that helps patients with pets. Volunteers in this group walk patients' dogs and take care of their pets when they cannot do so themselves. Keeping pets clean is essential to ensure they do not spread disease to their owners.

Families of AIDS patients need support, too, to help them understand how to best help their loved one. They may also need help in dealing with the grief that will come with the patient's death. Such support is provided by Mothers of AIDS Patients (MAP). This organization has chapters across the country. MAP was founded in 1985 by three women, each of whom had lost a child to AIDS.

*Rock star Elton John (right) is joined on stage by Ryan White (left) and Jason Robertson (center), both of whom have AIDS, during a concert to raise funds for AIDS patients. Many celebrities have offered their talents to raise money for AIDS research and to help offset the enormous medical costs incurred by AIDS patients.*

AIDS is an expensive disease to have. The lifetime medical-care costs for just one patient can reach 100 thousand dollars or more. Health insurance policies generally cover most medical costs for the treatment of AIDS. However, between 50 and 70 percent of all AIDS patients do not have such insurance. Many lost this coverage when they became too sick to work: Consequently, a great number of people with AIDS are dependent on government or state-run programs to cover their medical expenses.

Daily living expenses can also be a problem when AIDS patients become too sick to work. Many are fairly young and have not been able to save enough money to exist long without a job. For these people, financial assistance is often available through one of the following government programs: Social Security Disability (SSD) or Supplemental Security Income (SSI). The amounts of money available through these programs, however, are usually much less than the person would earn working.

A number of private foundations have contributed large sums of money to develop programs to help persons with AIDS. These include the Ford Foundation, the Rockefeller Foundation, and the Robert Wood Johnson Foundation.

Financial assistance, however, cannot help AIDS patients in one very important area. It cannot stop discrimination.

## Discrimination

Some people discriminate against people with AIDS because they have a basic dislike for those in high-risk groups (homosexual men, IV drug users, and prostitutes). Others feel AIDS patients and HIV carriers are a threat to their health and should be avoided. Some have even proposed that infected people should be quarantined (isolated) to protect the rest of society.

Public health officials are opposed to quarantining and other actions that would discriminate against people who are infected with HIV. The officials believe that confidentiality (keeping private the names of those who are HIV-positive) will help, not hinder, the fight against AIDS. If people in high-risk groups think their names might be revealed, they will not go in for testing or seek treatment if they are sick, these officials say. Current policy is that local health departments do not use names when reporting AIDS cases to the Centers for Disease Control. Instead, the person's date of birth is used along with other information in code.

Infected people fear they might be discriminated against if their health condition is made known. Some fear loss of employment, and with it, loss of health insurance. Presently, the federal government, and some private companies, have anti-discrimination policies that provide job protection to people with AIDS and those infected with HIV. These people cannot be fired for health reasons as long as they are able to do their jobs.

## Barring children with AIDS from school

Some schools have barred children with AIDS from attending classes. Usually this has happened because parents of other students were worried that their children might get the disease. They didn't know, or didn't believe, that AIDS is *not* transmitted through breathing, coughing, touching, or hugging.

In some cases, the parents of the child with AIDS have gone to court to get their son or daughter admitted to school. This is what happened with Ryan White, a teenager with AIDS living in Indiana. Ryan, a hemophiliac, was diagnosed with AIDS at the age of twelve. After learning of his illness, school administrators in his home town of Kokomo refused to let him attend school. Instead, they hooked him up to a classroom by television. Ryan's mother Jeanne decided to go to court to get her son admitted to classes. She won, but parent protests forced Ryan to return home after only one day at school.

Jeanne eventually decided to move Ryan and his sister to the little town of Cicero, twenty-five miles away. Ryan was very ill when the family moved. He suffered from chills and nausea and weighed only fifty-four pounds. School officials in Cicero had a different attitude toward Ryan. They developed a plan that would help ease his admission to school. Before Ryan started classes, all students were required to attend a special two-hour class on AIDS. AIDS information was also sent home for parents to read. By Ryan's first day of school, everyone was well informed. They knew that no one's life was at risk. Ryan was happily surprised when he was welcomed and accepted by everyone.

## Ryan's courage

Today, Ryan is seventeen. He has many good friends at school and in the community. In addition, his health has improved dramatically since moving to Cicero. He enjoys visiting other schools to tell young people his story and the facts about AIDS. His courage has won him much admiration and many new friends, including a few celebrities. Greg Louganis, the Olympic diving champ, and rock star Elton John have both become Ryan's special pals. A national television special about Ryan's life aired in January 1989.

Fortunately, more and more schools are today accepting children like Ryan. One recent poll showed that 68 percent of the adults questioned felt that children with AIDS should be allowed to attend school. The CDC has developed special school admission guidelines for these students to ensure the safety of everyone.

CHAPTER SIX

# AIDS in the Next Decade

Many diseases have plagued the world throughout its history. One famous epidemic, the Black Death (the Plague), struck Europe and Asia during the fourteenth century and eventually killed 75 million people. More recently, a deadly kind of flu killed 22 million people worldwide between 1918 and 1920. AIDS, the world's most recent epidemic, may be the first one to be 100 percent fatal to those who acquire the disease.

### How widespread is AIDS?

The fact that AIDS is a worldwide health problem is reflected in the 152,000 cases of the disease that had been reported in 149 countries by April 1989. This reported total, however, does not reflect what actually exists, experts say. According to the World Health Organization (WHO), only about half of all AIDS cases are officially reported. This is partly because some countries where AIDS is widespread are very poor and have little money to spend on public health. In Tanzania, Africa, for example, the total health budget for 1988 was one dollar for each person in the country. Tanzania and other countries do not have the funds to provide adequate medical programs. Nor do they have funds to set up a system to keep track of AIDS cases.

In Africa, AIDS is mainly spread through heterosexual (male-female) sex. As a result, equal numbers of men and women have the disease. Because many women are involved, a great number of infected babies are also being born. (Some researchers believe as many as 10 percent of all African babies may have the virus at birth.) Many African people do not read, and consequently do not know the facts about AIDS transmission. This lack of knowledge has allowed the disease to spread quickly in many countries in Africa. A few areas of the world, however, appear to be relatively untouched by the virus. For example, as of October 1988, there had been only sixty-five cases of AIDS reported in the Soviet Union and only one death attributed to the disease.

Although most cases of AIDS have occurred in the United States, Africa, and western Europe, the disease has been found in almost all of the world's countries. Experts estimate that a million people worldwide will develop AIDS by 1994. To stop this epidemic will take a worldwide effort, the experts say. Other diseases, such as smallpox, have been conquered when such an effort has been made. As the result of a worldwide vaccination program, smallpox is no longer a threat. No cases of the disease have been reported since 1977. The fight to eliminate AIDS, however, will not be as easy. So far, the virus has been able to outsmart the world's best scientific researchers.

## Controlling a plague

In an effort to control this modern-day plague, countries have begun to pool their knowledge about AIDS. In 1985, the first international conference on AIDS was held in Atlanta, Georgia. Other conferences followed in Paris, France (1986), Washington, D.C. (1987), and Stockholm, Sweden (1988). Over seven thousand people attended the Stockholm meeting and many more were expected at the most recent conference (1989) in Montreal, Canada. Another important gathering took place in January 1988 when the First World Summit

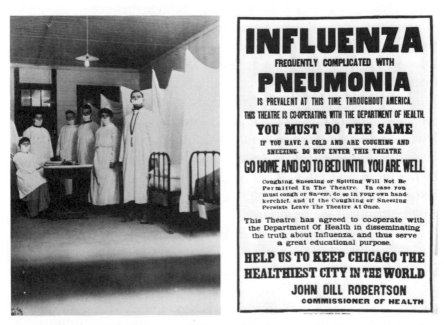

*As with the AIDS epidemic today, people have worked together in the past to fight disease epidemics. The picture on the left shows the staff of an early twentieth-century epidemic ward. On the right is a poster urging theatergoers with flu symptoms to cooperate with public health authorities in preventing an epidemic.*

on AIDS convened in London, England. This international gathering drew representatives from 122 countries. Health officials and others who attend these sessions come together to exchange information on studies being done around the world. So far, there have been more questions than answers.

Why do some persons with AIDS die within a year of being diagnosed while others live on for five years or more? Why do some people resist infection despite repeated exposure to HIV? Are there variations in cells that make blacks or Hispanics more vulnerable than Caucasians? These are some of the questions being asked by those involved in the fight against AIDS.

In hundreds of laboratories in dozens of countries, researchers are working hard to unravel the riddle of AIDS. HIV is a very complicated virus, but this characteristic may actually be helpful to scientists. Because it is so complex, there may be more ways the scientists can interfere with the virus's ability to infect human cells. Despite the combined efforts of the world's researchers, however, answers to the riddle will not come quickly. Finding a cure for those who suffer from AIDS may not be possible, experts say. They also believe a vaccine to protect healthy people may be ten years or more away.

Even though some AIDS experiments fail, scientists feel the knowledge gained about the immune system as a result of these studies will benefit other areas of medicine. Ultimately, it may prove helpful in the treatment of other viral diseases and perhaps even of cancer.

## Finding a vaccine

The purpose of a vaccine is to protect the body from attack by a germ it has never encountered before. The vaccine does this by stimulating the immune system to make antibodies against the germ before the germ actually invades the body. If the body has these advance weapons, it will not be caught off guard. Normally, when the immune system encounters a new germ in the bloodstream, it must hurry to produce antibodies to destroy the germ before it can cause disease. Sometimes it can't work fast enough to stop this from happening, and the person becomes ill. If the disease is particularly severe, the immune system may be overpowered. Then the infected person may become seriously ill and possibly die. A person who has previously received vaccine against the disease, however, is protected because antibodies are ready to pounce on the germ as soon as it enters the bloodstream. By destroying the invader swiftly, antibodies are able to preserve the person's health.

In order to vaccinate a person against AIDS, a harmless part of

HIV must be injected into the person's bloodstream. This bit of virus must be enough to stimulate the production of antibodies, but not enough to make the person sick. That is, the vaccine must give the body a hint of what to expect, but not give the whole disease. Researchers around the world are working on a safe way to do this.

The first reported test of a vaccine on humans was by Dr. Daniel Zagury of the Pierre and Marie Curie Institute of the University of Paris in 1987. After conducting successful experiments with animals, Zagury, along with eleven others, volunteered to be injected with an experimental vaccine. It was much like the one used to vaccinate against smallpox, but the new vaccine also contained a part of HIV's outer protein shell. Later a similar vaccine was administered to six volunteers in a United States experiment. In both studies, all participants produced antibodies to HIV and none experienced serious side effects. Further tests are needed to determine if the antibodies produced by their bodies can provide protection against HIV infection.

## Searching for a cure

The search for an effective AIDS vaccine has been complicated by HIV's ability to change its shape, or mutate. The effectiveness of an AIDS vaccine is based on one thing—it must be able to stimulate the production of antibodies that perfectly match the shape of HIV. This perfect match enables the antibodies to destroy the virus when it enters the body. If HIV makes changes in its outer appearance, however, the antibodies will no longer be a perfect match. Consequently, they may not be able to destroy the invader. The vaccine will then lose its power to prevent infection. Therefore, more than one AIDS vaccine may be required to provide protection against the various mutations of HIV. In one laboratory study, a single person's blood was found to have seventeen such mutations.

The situation has become even more complicated with the discovery of a new and different virus that can also cause AIDS. French scientists in West Africa discovered the new virus, called HIV-2, while

*Dr. Daniel Zagury of the Curie Institute at the University of Paris developed an AIDS vaccine that he tested on himself and others. Dr. Zagury believes the vaccine will successfully stop the spread of AIDS.*

searching for mutations of the first AIDS virus, now called HIV-1. Although HIV-2 is widespread in West Africa, it is rare in the United States. In this country, the first case of AIDS caused by HIV-2 was diagnosed in December 1987. The patient was a West African living in New Jersey whose blood had tested negative for HIV-1, but positive for HIV-2.

## Other efforts

In dealing with a tricky virus, researchers have come up with a few tricks themselves. For example, scientists have found the exact spot on the T-cell where the virus attaches itself. HIV is able to enter the cell at this spot because the protein molecule here is a perfect match for the virus's outer protein shell. In the laboratory, protein fragments have been created that are exact copies of the T-cell's outer protein molecule. The scientists are using these fragments as decoys to trick the virus. When the virus sees a fragment, it thinks it is a T-cell, and locks onto it. The fragment is of little use to the virus, however, because it is not a cell. It does not have the material the virus needs to reproduce itself.

Other laboratory tests have been done using a protein that has been combined with a poisonous substance. In these tests, the protein has been able to kill cells infected with HIV but does not harm healthy cells. If approved for use in humans, regular treatments may be able to keep HIV under control in infected persons who have not yet developed symptoms.

## Research experiments

Important AIDS research experiments are being conducted at the Salk Institute in San Diego, California, and the Louis Pasteur Institute in Paris, France. Some of the world's most eminent scientists are connected with these two research facilities. Dr. Jonas Salk, founder of the Salk Institute, developed the first vaccine against polio. The Pasteur Institute's Dr. Luc Montagnier, along with Dr. Robert Gallo of the U.S. National Cancer Institute, is credited with identifying HIV as the virus that causes AIDS.

One of the real heroes in the war against AIDS may turn out to be a special breed of mouse. So far, animal studies with HIV have been of limited use since animals do not develop AIDS. But researchers now have at their disposal an animal that is different from

*Dr. Robert Gallo, laboratory chief of the National Cancer Institute, identified HIV as the virus that causes AIDS.*

other laboratory animals. Scientists have been successful in transplanting human immune systems into a special breed of mouse that is born with no immune system of its own. Since the mice have transplanted human white blood cells in their bodies, it is hoped they will respond to HIV infection in much the same way as humans. Thus, the mice will be helpful in the testing of experimental drugs and vaccines.

## AIDS in the 1990s

How much scientific progress has been made since 1981 in the war against AIDS? In one sense, the world's scientists appear to have made more progress than the world's educators. Despite massive educational campaigns, large numbers of people remain uninformed or unconcerned. Ignorance continues to be a major obstacle in controlling the spread of HIV. Generally speaking, people who are not directly involved in a problem tend to ignore it. AIDS, however, is a problem no one can afford to ignore. It is going to be in our society for many years. Even if all infection were to stop today, the millions in the world who are already infected will continue to develop the disease.

Although most people in the United States today do not know anyone with AIDS, sooner or later they will. This disease will eventually touch each American personally, if not first-hand, then certainly through the experience of a friend or relative. While researchers continue to look for a cure and a vaccine, individuals must take responsibility for protecting themselves against AIDS.

When people are informed, infection does not happen accidentally. People choose their sex partners and whether they will participate in high-risk behaviors such as shooting drugs. By making the right choices, individuals can protect themselves against disease while helping to create a world that is both free from fear and free from infection.

# Glossary

**abstinence:** Refraining from sex.

**Acquired Immune Deficiency Syndrome (AIDS):** A viral disease that weakens the immune system and leaves the body open to other serious infections.

**activist:** A person who vigorously supports a cause.

**AIDS dementia complex:** A brain disorder associated with AIDS.

**AIDS-Related Complex (ARC):** A condition caused by HIV infection that is milder than AIDS; also called HIV-related illness.

**AL-721:** A nutritional supplement, made from eggs and soybeans, used by many AIDS patients to improve their health.

**anal intercourse:** Sexual activity that involves a man inserting his penis into his partner's anus.

**antibody:** A protective substance produced by the body to attack an invading microorganism.

**anus:** The body opening between the buttocks through which the bowels are emptied.

**asymptomatic carrier:** A person who carries a disease-causing microorganism, but does not have symptoms of the disease.

**autologous transfusion:** Blood donated by a person for his or her own use at a later time.

**AZT (azidothymidine):** A drug used in the treatment of AIDS that is able to interfere with HIV's ability to reproduce in host cells; another name for zidovudine.

**B-lymphocyte cells:** The white blood cells that produce antibodies.

**bisexual:** A person who is sexually attracted to both men and women.

**casual contact:** Non-sexual contact between people, such as handshaking and hugging.

**chemotherapy:** The treatment of cancer and other serious conditions with strong chemicals.

**condom:** A rubber sheath that fits over a man's penis. The condom is designed to trap semen released from the penis and prevent pregnancy and sexually-transmitted diseases.

**cryptosporidiosis:** A type of diarrhea caused by an intestinal parasite; often seen in AIDS patients.

**ejaculation:** The release of semen from the penis.

**encephalitis:** A disease of the brain.

**Factor VIII:** The blood product used to treat hemophilia.

**fungus:** A tiny form of plant (e.g., yeast) that is capable of causing infection in humans.

**genitals:** The sexual organs.

**hemophilia:** An inherited condition in which the person's blood lacks substances needed for clotting.

**herpes simplex:** A virus that normally causes cold sores and fever blisters but can cause severe infection in AIDS patients and others with weakened immune systems.

**heterosexual:** A person who prefers to have sex with a member of the opposite sex.

**HIV antibody test:** A blood test that can determine whether a person has been infected with HIV.

**homosexual:** A person who is sexually attracted to members of his or her own sex.

**host cell:** A living cell that a virus penetrates in order to get materials it needs to reproduce.

**human immunodeficiency virus (HIV):** The virus that causes AIDS.

**immune system:** The body system that protects a person from disease.

**intravenous (IV) drug:** A drug that is injected by needle into a vein.

**Kaposi's sarcoma (KS):** A skin cancer that is commonly seen in AIDS patients.

**macrophages:** White blood cells that eat viruses and other germs.

**marker:** A sign or indicator that a condition is present; Kaposi's sarcoma is a marker of AIDS.

**microorganisms:** Tiny organisms such as viruses and bacteria that can invade the human body.

**monogamous (relationship):** A relationship in which two people have sex only with each other.

**mucous membrane:** Moist body tissue such as the tissue that lines the vagina and anus.

**mutate:** To change or alter.

**mycobacterium avium-intracellulare (MAI):** A lung disease, resembling tuberculosis.

**opportunistic infections:** Infections that primarily afflict persons with weakened immune systems.

**oral candida:** A fungal infection of the tongue and mouth that is commonly seen in AIDS patients.

**oral sex:** Sexual activity involving oral contact (mouth and tongue) with the partner's genitals.

**penis:** The male sexual organ.

**plasma:** The liquid portion of blood.

**pneumocystis carinii pneumonia (PCP):** A serious lung infection seen primarily in AIDS patients.

**prostitutes:** Persons who provide sex in return for money.

**protected sex:** Sexual intercourse using a condom to prevent contact with infected body fluids.

**saliva:** The body fluid in the mouth.

**semen:** The body fluid released from the man's penis during sexual activity.

**shooting gallery:** A secluded place like an alley or abandoned building where many drug users gather to take drugs.

**side effects:** Undesirable symptoms produced by a medication.

**T-cells:** Specialized white blood cells that help protect the body against disease but are capable of being attacked by HIV.

**thrush:** Another name for oral candida, a fungal infection.

**vaccine:** A substance that stimulates production of antibodies against a disease-causing microorganism.

**vagina:** A part of the female sexual organs. The canal that leads from outside the body to the uterus.

**vaginal secretions:** Body fluids present in the vagina and vaginal area.

**virus:** A tiny disease-causing microorganism that depends on a living cell to survive and reproduce.

**zidovudine:** Another name for AZT, a drug used to treat AIDS.

# Organizations to Contact

**American Red Cross**—local chapters
(check phone directory)

**Centers for Disease Control**
Office of Public Inquiries
Bldg. 1, Room B-63
1600 Clifton Road
Atlanta, GA 30333

**Mothers of AIDS Patients (MAP)**
P.O. Box 3132
San Diego, CA 92103

**U.S. Public Health Service**
Public Affairs Office
Hubert H. Humphrey Bldg., Room 725-H
200 Independence Ave. SW
Washington, D.C. 20201

## Telephone Hotlines (no charge)

National Drug Abuse Hotline:   1-800-662-HELP

National AIDS Hotline:          1-800-342-AIDS (English)
                                1-800-342-SIDA (Spanish)

**Note:** Many informational pamphlets prepared by the U.S. Public Health Service and the American Red Cross are available free upon request by calling the AIDS Hotline number listed above.

# Suggestions for Further Reading

Nigel Hawkes, *AIDS*. New York: Gloucester Press, 1987.

Margaret O. Hyde and Elizabeth H. Forsyth, *Know About AIDS*. New York: Walker and Co., 1987.

C. Everett Koop, *Surgeon General's Report on Acquired Immune Deficiency Syndrome*. Washington, D.C.: U.S. Department of Health and Human Services, 1986.

Ethan A. Lerner, *Understanding AIDS*. Minneapolis: Lerner Publications Co., 1987.

Suzanne LeVert, *AIDS, In Search of a Killer*. New York: J. Messner, 1987.

*Newsweek*, "More Facts, Less Hope," June 27, 1988, pp. 46-47.

*People Weekly*, "AIDS, A Diary of the Plague in America," August 3, 1987, pp. 61-79.

*People Weekly*, "The Quiet Victories of Ryan White," May 30, 1988, pp. 88-96.

Cindy Ruskin, *The Quilt: Stories from the NAMES Project*. New York: Simon & Schuster, 1988.

Alvin Silverstein and Virginia B. Silverstein, *AIDS: Deadly Threat*. Hillside, NJ: Enslow Publishers, 1986.

Gloria Steinem, "Small Steps in Fighting AIDS," *Newsweek*, June 27, 1988, p. 8.

# Index

# Acknowledgments

I am especially indebted to the following persons for the valuable contributions they made to this book: Rick Anderson, David and Suzi Mandell, Marguerite M. Jackson, Director, Medical Center Epidemiology Unit, University of California, San Diego, and Edward S. Fletcher, Health Services Director, San Diego Unified School District. I am also deeply grateful to my friends and family for providing me with daily helpings of love, support, and encouragement. Special thanks go to LoVerne Brown, my favorite writer, who also happens to be my mother.

# Picture Credits

Photos supplied by Dixon & Turner Research Associates, Bethesda, Maryland
Cover Illustration by MASH 101, San Diego, California
AP/Wide World Photos, 9, 11, 14, 16, 40, 41, 46, 47, 51, 57, 58
Clay Bennett. Reprinted by permission of Copley News Service, 30
Centers for Disease Control, 20, 21, 24, 25, 29, 54
By permission of Johnny Hart and NAS, Inc., 38
Steve Kelley. Reprinted with permission, 8
Minnesota AIDS Media Consortium, 48
National Institute for Allergy and Infectious Disease, National Institutes of Health, 20
National Cancer Institute, 68
National Library of Medicine, 64
Reuters/Bettmann Newsphotos, 13, 67
The San Diego Union, Bruce K. Huff, 36
UPI/Bettmann Newsphotos, 42, 49

# About the Author

Jonnie Wilson is senior editor for the San Diego Unified School District. A writer and editor for 16 years, she has won many awards for her journalistic work from professional organizations, including the San Diego Press Club, the California Newspaper Publishers Association, and the Society of Professional Journalists.